Managing Editor
Ina Massler Levin, M.A.

Editor
Eric Migliaccio

Contributing Editors
Sarah Smith
Kristine Smith

Creative Director
Karen J. Goldfluss, M.S. Ed.

Cover Design
Tony Carrillo / Marilyn Goldberg

Teacher Created Resources
12621 Western Avenue
Garden Grove, CA 92841
www.teachercreated.com

ISBN: 978-1-4206-5968-9

©2007 *Teacher Created Resources*
Reprinted, 2024 (PO605697)

Made in U.S.A.

This book belongs to

____

Ready·Set·Learn

Get Ready to Learn!

Get ready, get set, and go! Boost your child's learning with this exciting series of books. Geared to help children practice and master many needed skills, the *Ready Set Learn* books are bursting with 64 pages of learning fun. Use these books for . . .

 enrichment    skills reinforcement    extra practice

With their smaller size, the *Ready Set Learn* books fit easily in children's hands, backpacks, and book bags. All your child needs to get started are pencils, crayons, and colored pencils.

A full sheet of colorful stickers is included. Use these stickers for . . .

- decorating pages

- rewarding outstanding effort

- keeping track of completed pages

Celebrate your child's progress by using these stickers on the reward chart located on the inside cover. The blue-ribbon sticker fits perfectly on the certificate on page 64.

With *Ready Set Learn* and a little encouragement, your child will be on the fast track to learning fun!

Baking a Cake

Directions: Look at the picture. Read the story.

I baked a cake in my oven. I ate the cake. It tasted good.

Directions: Read the questions. Circle the correct pictures.

1. What was baked?

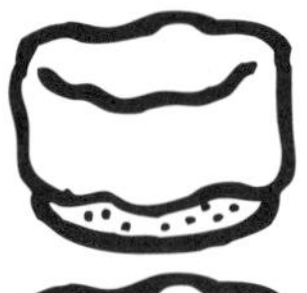 

2. Where was it baked?

3. Who ate the cake?

In the Garden

Directions: Look at the picture. Read the story.

Joey mows the grass. He uses the hose to water the plants. Joey is a good gardener.

Directions: Read the questions. Circle the correct pictures.

1. What does Joey mow?

2. What does Joey water?

My Pet Dog

Directions: Look at the picture. Read the story.

My dog can fetch an egg from a hen. The hen may peck, but my pet can run like a jet!

Directions: Fill in the missing word in each sentence.

1. The _________________________ can fetch an egg.

2. The _________________________ can run like a jet.

Jack and Jill

Directions: Look at the picture. Read the poem.

Jack and Jill

Went up a hill

To fetch a pail of water;

Jack fell down

And broke his crown,

And Jill came tumbling

after.

Directions: Answer the questions.

1. Who went up a hill?

____

- -

2. What happened to Jack?

____

- -

____

- -

____

A Bath

Directions: Look at the picture. Read the story.

I scrub myself in the tub. A bug looks at me.
I splash on the rug. The bug jumps in the tub.

Directions: Fill in the missing word in each sentence.

1. The person is in the _______________.

2. The _______________ jumps in the tub.

Bedtime

Directions: Read the story.

> At bedtime, my father reads a story to me and tucks me in my covers. Then we tell each other about our day. He says that he is proud of me. I always have sweet dreams!

Directions: Answer the questions.

1. What is the first thing the father does?

____

2. What does the child tell the father?

____

3. How does the child sleep?

____

Giraffes

Directions: Read the passage below. Answer the questions at the bottom of the page by filling in the correct bubbles.

Giraffes live on the grasslands of Africa. They are known for their long legs and necks. Giraffes are so tall that they feed on leaves at the tops of trees. Giraffes use their long tongues to pull the leaves off the trees. In order for giraffes to get water, they have to spread their front legs apart and bend way down low. Although giraffes have few enemies, they are always on the lookout for danger. They have good eyesight and hearing to help them.

1. What are giraffes known for?
   - ⓐ their patterns
   - ⓑ their long legs and necks
   - ⓒ their good eyesight

2. What does the word *feed* mean in this passage?
   - ⓐ eat
   - ⓑ seed
   - ⓒ collect

3. How do giraffes get leaves?
   - ⓐ from a caregiver
   - ⓑ collect them on the ground
   - ⓒ pull them off the trees

4. Why do giraffes have to spread their legs when drinking water?
   - ⓐ their height
   - ⓑ to look for danger
   - ⓒ to reach the leaves

Penguins

Directions: Read the passage below. Answer the questions at the bottom of the page by filling in the correct bubbles.

Penguins are unusual birds. They have feathers, but they cannot fly. They are very good at swimming. In fact, penguins spend most of their time swimming. The water is where penguins find their food. They really enjoy eating fish, squid, and krill. There are not many birds like the penguin!

1. What is a penguin's body covering?

    (a) fur   (b) feathers   (c) scales

2. What do penguins like to eat?

    (a) fish   (b) insects   (c) plants

3. What is the main idea of the paragraph?

    (a) Penguins are good swimmers.

    (b) Penguins find their food in water.

    (c) Penguins are unusual birds.

An Odd Fish

A seahorse does not swim like other fish do. It moves through the water like a rocking horse. Its head looks like a horse's head. It uses its long **snout** to suck up food.

The seahorse has a hard body that feels like bones. It can wrap its tail around a piece of seaweed. It hides there so that sea turtles and sharks do not find it.

A male seahorse gives birth to the babies! The female puts her eggs into his pouch. He carries the eggs for six weeks. Then the little babies pop out and swim away.

An Odd Fish *(cont.)*

Directions: Fill in the bubble next to the right answer.

1. A seahorse's head looks like

    ⓐ a horse's.

    ⓑ seaweed.

2. What happens last?

    ⓐ The male carries the eggs.

    ⓑ The babies swim away.

3. What makes a seahorse different from other fish?

    ⓐ It swims in a different way.

    ⓑ It is a horse, not a fish.

4. A snout is

    ⓐ an ear.

    ⓑ a nose and mouth.

5. Why does the seahorse hide from sea turtles and sharks?

    ⓐ They want to eat the seahorse.

    ⓑ They are playing hide and seek.

A Whale of a Time

Dolphins are little whales. But most whales are big. The blue whale is the **largest** animal on Earth.

Whales live in the sea. They swim in groups. They make sounds to "talk." All whales have a hole on top of their heads. They do not stay under the water all of the time. They need to come up for air. When they go back under the water, the hole shuts.

Whales are mammals, just like us. They are smart. They can learn tricks. You may see a dolphin at a sea park. They are fun to watch!

A Whale of a Time *(cont.)*

Directions: Fill in the bubble next to the right answer.

1. Most whales are

   ⓐ big.

   ⓑ small.

2. What happens first?

   ⓐ The whale does a trick.

   ⓑ The man teaches the whale a trick.

3. How is a whale different from a fish?

   ⓐ All fish live in fresh water.

   ⓑ A fish is not a mammal.

4. What word means the same as *largest*?

   ⓐ biggest

   ⓑ weakest

5. What trick might a sea park whale do?

   ⓐ jump through a hoop

   ⓑ sing a song

Plants Are Important

All plants need water, air, and light. Plants do not eat. They use the light from the sun to make their own food. That is why a plant always grows towards the sun. Plants make the food in their leaves. Then they store the food in their stems and roots. They use this food on **gloomy** days when the sun is covered by clouds.

If there were no plants, there would be no life on Earth. Plants start every food chain. An animal eats the plant. Or it eats the seeds or fruit of the plant. Then another animal eats that animal. Some animals eat both plants and animals.

Plants Are Important *(cont.)*

Directions: Fill in the bubble next to the right answer.

1. Plants cannot

ⓐ eat food.

ⓑ use food.

2. What happens first?

ⓐ A plant uses food from its roots.

ⓑ A plant makes food from the sun.

3. Where do plants get water?

ⓐ the ground

ⓑ the store

4. *Gloomy* means

ⓐ dark.

ⓑ bright.

5. Picture a bush growing in the shade of a tree. How does it look?

ⓐ Most of the bush's branches are growing towards the shade.

ⓑ Most of the bush's branches are growing away from the shade.

Water

You know that there is more water than land on Earth. But did you know that there are two kinds of water? There is fresh water, and there is salt water. There is much more salt water than fresh water on Earth. Salt water is in the sea. We cannot drink it. It would make us ill. But most sea animals must stay in salt water. If they are put in fresh water, they die.

Lakes and rivers hold fresh water. Rain, snow, and ice are **forms** of fresh water. Many animals and all plants and people need fresh water. Without water there could be no life on Earth.

Water *(cont.)*

Directions: Fill in the bubble next to the right answer.

1. What kind of water can people drink?

ⓐ salt water

ⓑ fresh water

2. What happens last?

ⓐ A person gets sick.

ⓑ A person drinks salt water.

3. Why do freshwater animals have to stay in fresh water?

ⓐ because salt water is different and not good for them

ⓑ because there isn't enough salt water for them

4. The word *forms* means

ⓐ kinds.

ⓑ spots.

5. What happens when snow melts?

ⓐ It turns into salt water.

ⓑ It turns into fresh water.

Air

Air is all around us. We cannot see it. But it takes up space.
It takes up space inside of a balloon. When the balloon
pops, the air **rushes** out.

When air moves outside, we call it wind. Warm air goes up.
Cold air goes down. Wind, warm air, and cold air make our
weather change.

We must take care to keep our air clean. We need to breathe
air. All plants and animals do. Even fish breathe air. Their
gills take air out of the water.

Air *(cont.)*

Directions: Fill in the bubble next to the right answer.

1. What needs air?

ⓐ just animals

ⓑ both plants and animals

2. What happens last?

ⓐ The balloon hits something sharp.

ⓑ The air goes out of the balloon.

3. When the wind blows,

ⓐ warm and cold air move around outdoors.

ⓑ no rain can fall.

4. *Rushes* means

ⓐ moves slowly.

ⓑ moves quickly.

5. Why do we need clean air?

ⓐ If we breathe dirty air, it may make us sick.

ⓑ Clean air costs less than dirty air.

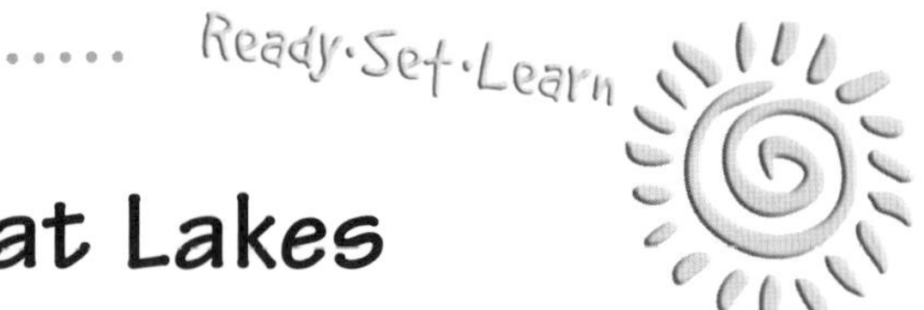

The Great Lakes

The five Great Lakes are very big. They can be seen from space! The lakes hold a lot of fresh water. One is Lake Superior. It is the second-biggest lake in the world.

The lakes are between America and Canada. On one side of four lakes is America. On the other side is Canada. But this is not true for one lake. Lake Michigan is inside the U.S.

The Great Lakes are **linked**. A ship can move from one to the other. Many ships go from lake to lake. They bring things to people. These ships may even go out to the sea. Then they can go to other countries.

The Great Lakes (cont.)

Directions: Fill in the bubble next to the right answer.

1. What is the second-biggest lake in the world?

ⓐ Lake Erie

ⓑ Lake Superior

2. What two countries share the Great Lakes?

ⓐ America and Canada

ⓑ America and Mexico

3. Can a ship from the sea reach the Great Lakes?

ⓐ no

ⓑ yes

4. *Linked* means

ⓐ stacked.

ⓑ joined.

5. Picture a ship bringing things to people in the Great Lakes. What is the ship made of?

ⓐ paper

ⓑ metal

The Desert

A desert is hot and dry. Very little rain falls. Wind blows the sand. This forms dunes. Each day the sun heats up the desert. Then at night the desert gets very cold!

Many kinds of animals and plants live in a desert. Most animals sleep in the day. They come out at night to hunt. Some animals, like the camel, store water in their bodies. They can go for weeks without a drink. Cactus plants store water, too. Their sharp **needles** keep the animals from taking it.

Few people live in the desert. They need more water than they can find there.

The Desert *(cont.)*

Directions: Fill in the bubble next to the right answer.

1. What kind of plant can store water?

ⓐ a cactus

ⓑ grass

2. Is the desert hot at all times?

ⓐ no

ⓑ yes

3. Why do some plants and animals store water?

ⓐ because it snows in the desert

ⓑ because it is dry in the desert

4. Why are most desert animals awake at night?

ⓐ They cannot see during the day.

ⓑ It is cool enough to come out then.

5. Picture a desert during the day. What do you see?

ⓐ lots of animals

ⓑ lots of sand

Don't Play with Fire

Be careful near fire. Clothes and paper burn easily. Keep away from hot stoves and grills. Never play with matches or a lighter.

If you ever catch on fire, do not run! Drop to the ground. Roll around until the fire goes out. Then get help. Burns are bad. You must see a doctor right away.

Have a smoke **alarm** in your home. If you hear it, get out! Fire can move fast. Smoke can, too. Smoke rises, so stay low. Try not to breathe smoke. If you cannot reach a door, go out a window.

Stay back. Firefighters will put out the fire.

Don't Play with Fire *(cont.)*

Directions: Fill in the bubble next to the right answer.

1. What catches fire easily?

ⓐ green grass

ⓑ paper

2. If you hear a smoke alarm, what should you do first?

ⓐ Call the firefighters.

ⓑ Get out of the house.

3. The word *alarm* means

ⓐ a noise that warns.

ⓑ the sound of a horn.

4. Why shouldn't you run if you catch on fire?

ⓐ Running is too hard to do.

ⓑ Running would not put out the fire.

5. Picture a house on fire. What is coming out of its windows?

ⓐ smoke

ⓑ bugs

The Fourth of July

We see fireworks on the Fourth of July. There are **parades**.
Most people have the day off. Why? It is America's
birthday.

At one time a king ruled America. He lived across the sea.
The people did not like this. They wanted to make their own
laws. They wanted to be free. So they told the king. It was
July 4, 1776.

The king got mad. He sent men to fight. When the war was
over, America was free.

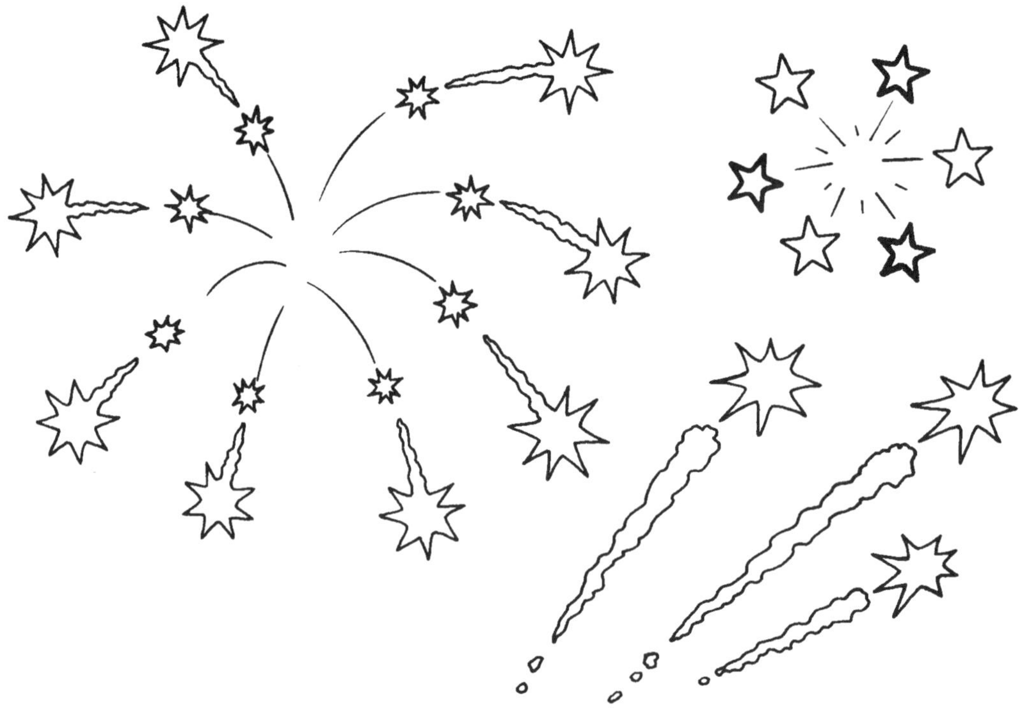

The Fourth of July *(cont.)*

Directions: Fill in the bubble next to the right answer.

1. On July 4, 1776,

   ⓐ a king started to rule America.

   ⓑ the people told the king that they were free.

2. What happened first?

   ⓐ The people had parades and fireworks on July 4th.

   ⓑ The people fought to be free.

3. America's birthday is July 4th because

   ⓐ that is the day that the king lost the war.

   ⓑ that is the day that the people said they were free.

4. During *parades*

   ⓐ bands play music.

   ⓑ people run.

5. What would have happened if America lost the fight?

   ⓐ The people would have made their own laws.

   ⓑ The king would have stayed the ruler.

The First Thanksgiving

In 1620 the Pilgrims left England. They wanted their own land. They sailed in a ship called the *Mayflower*. When they reached America, they named their new home Plymouth.

The first winter was hard. There wasn't much to eat. Half of the people died. In the spring, Native Americans found them. They gave the Pilgrims corn seeds. They told them where to fish and dig for clams.

By that fall the people had lots of food. They had a big **feast**. They asked the Native Americans to come. They ate for three days! It was the first Thanksgiving.

The First Thanksgiving *(cont.)*

Directions: Fill in the bubble next to the right answer.

1. What was the name of the ship the Pilgrims sailed on?

  ⓐ *Plymouth*

  ⓑ *Mayflower*

2. What happened last?

  ⓐ The people almost starved to death.

  ⓑ The people met the Native Americans.

3. Did it help the Pilgrims when the Native Americans gave them corn seeds?

  ⓐ Yes, because then the Pilgrims had a crop of corn.

  ⓑ No, because the Pilgrims didn't know what to do with them.

4. The word *feast* means

  ⓐ meal.

  ⓑ wedding.

5. Why did the Pilgrims ask the Native Americans to come?

  ⓐ because the Native Americans had given them help

  ⓑ because they wanted to stop the war with the Native Americans

Keeping You Safe

Many people work to keep you safe. Your doctor wants to keep you well. When you are sick, your doctor may give you pills so you will get better.

The police make sure that no one breaks into your home. They keep watch so that no one hurts you.

Firefighters put out fires. If your home catches on fire, they come. They spray water from hoses. The fire will go out. Your home may be saved.

Ambulance workers hurry to you if you are hurt badly. They take care of you. They rush you to the **hospital**. They can save your life.

Keeping You Safe *(cont.)*

Directions: Fill in the bubble next to the right answer.

1. What do ambulance workers do?

ⓐ They take hurt or very sick people to a hospital.

ⓑ They use hoses to fight fires.

2. What happens last?

ⓐ A person calls the ambulance.

ⓑ The hurt child goes away in the ambulance.

4. A *hospital* is

ⓐ where the firefighters work.

ⓑ where doctors help people who are hurt.

5. Who do you call if someone broke into your home?

ⓐ the police

ⓑ the doctor

6. Picture a doctor's office. Who else works there?

ⓐ nurses

ⓑ police

The First Clothes

Long, long ago people had no clothes. They lived in warm places. They did not need clothes. But the people followed animals. So over time they moved to colder places. They did not like the cold. So after they killed an animal they put its skin around them. It was like a **blanket**. Then they felt warmer.

Over time they learned to make needles from bird bones. They made thread from strong grass. They cut the animal skins with sharp rocks or bones. Then they sewed the pieces together into the first clothes. The clothes kept the people warm.

The First Clothes *(cont.)*

Directions: Fill in the bubble next to the right answer.

1. What did the early people use for needles?

ⓐ bird bones

ⓑ strong grasses

2. What happened first?

ⓐ People used animal skins to stay warm.

ⓑ People did not wear clothes.

3. A *blanket* is

ⓐ clothes.

ⓑ something we cover up with.

4. Why did the people make animal skins into clothes?

ⓐ They did not know what else to do with the animal skins.

ⓑ The clothes stayed on better than the animal-skin blanket did.

5. Picture a person wearing some of the first clothes. What do you see on the clothes?

ⓐ fur

ⓑ buttons

The Dodos

Dodo birds had only one home. They lived on an island in the Indian Ocean. When **sailors** found their island, the birds were in big trouble. These birds could not fly. They were easy to catch. So the men ate them.

Pigs came on the ships. Sometimes the men could not catch them. Then the pigs stayed on the island. The pigs ate all of the dodo birds' eggs.

In 1680 the last dodo bird died. There are none of these birds left on Earth.

The Dodos *(cont.)*

Directions: Fill in the bubble next to the right answer.

1. Which animal died out?

ⓐ dodo birds

ⓑ pigs

2. What happened last?

ⓐ Sailors found the island.

ⓑ Pigs were loose on the island.

3. What made the dodo birds easy to catch?

ⓐ They could not fly.

ⓑ They could not run.

4. *Sailors* are

ⓐ the people who keep animals safe.

ⓑ the people who work on ships.

6. Picture a dodo bird's nest from long ago. Where is it?

ⓐ on the ground

ⓑ high up in a tree

Chewing the Cud

A deer is afraid when it is in an open field. It thinks that other animals might attack it. So it tears off big pieces of leaves and branches from bushes. But it does not chew them. It **swallows** them whole!

This food gets stored in a special part of the deer's stomach. When the deer is back in the woods, it feels safer. Then it brings up the stored food, or cud. The deer chews the cud. Chewing the cud breaks the food into little pieces. Then the deer's body can use it.

Chewing the Cud *(cont.)*

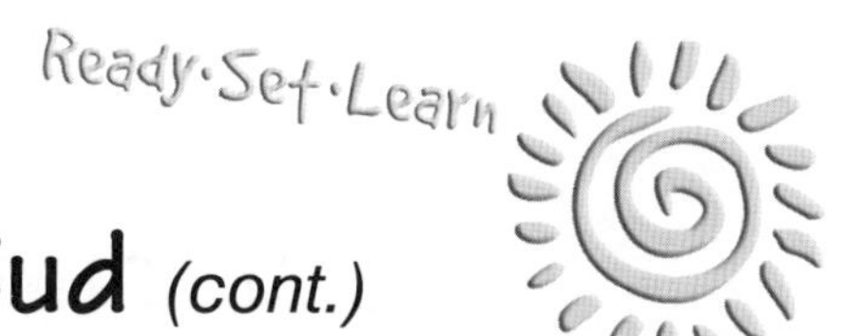

Directions: Fill in the bubble next to the right answer.

1. What is in cud?

ⓐ leaves and bark

ⓑ meat

2. What happens last?

ⓐ The deer grabs branches and leaves from a field.

ⓑ The deer chews the cud.

3. Why does the deer chew cud?

ⓐ to break its food into small pieces its body can use

ⓑ to keep its teeth from getting too long

4. *Swallows* means

ⓐ smells.

ⓑ gulps.

5. Which animal would a deer be afraid of?

ⓐ a wolf

ⓑ a rabbit

Our Sun and Moon

The sun is a big star. It gives heat and light to Earth. The sun is always shining. During our night, it shines on the other side of the world. The sun is there on cloudy days. The clouds hide it.

The moon gives off no light of its own. It only **reflects** the sun's light. Over the course of each month, the moon seems to change shape. Some of it seems to disappear. But the moon does not disappear or change shape. The whole moon is always there. We just see the part of the moon that the sun is lighting up as we look at it from our home on Earth. The part of the moon that we can see the sun light up can get smaller or larger as the moon goes around the Earth.

Our Sun and Moon *(cont.)*

Directions: Fill in the bubble next to the right answer.

1. Which looks like it changes shape?

ⓐ Earth

ⓑ the moon

2. What happens at the start of our day?

ⓐ The sun comes up.

ⓑ The sun goes down.

3. What would Earth be like without the sun?

ⓐ It would be hot and bright.

ⓑ It would be cold and dark.

4. *Reflects* means

ⓐ drinks up.

ⓑ throws back.

5. Which part of the moon can we see from our home on earth?

ⓐ the part that the sun lights up

ⓑ the part that is in the Earth's shadow

Native American Games and Toys

Have you ever played cat's cradle? That string game comes from Native Americans. Have you ever seen a lacrosse game? The players catch and throw a ball with nets on poles. That was a Native American game, too.

Native American boys and girls played other games, as well. They hid a small rock in a shoe and took turns guessing which shoe it was in. They made marks on flat stones. They used them as dice in **games of chance**.

The children played with toys. Little girls had dolls made of corncobs. Small boys had bows and arrows. They shot at logs. Older boys shot at moving hoops.

Native American Games and Toys (cont.)

Directions: Fill in the bubble next to the right answer.

1. What were the Native American girls' dolls made with?

  ⓐ flat stones

  ⓑ corncobs

2. How are today's toys different from the Native American toys?

  ⓐ No one plays with dolls or bows anymore.

  ⓑ Their toys were made of things found outside.

3. *Games of chance* are

  ⓐ games you win by luck.

  ⓑ games you win by skill.

4. Why did boys use bows and arrows?

  ⓐ because they didn't like the other games

  ⓑ because when they grew up, it would help them to hunt

5. Picture Native American children long ago. What are they doing?

  ⓐ playing with stones and sticks

  ⓑ pulling a wagon with toys in it

Stars

When you look up in the sky at night, what do you see? If it is a clear night, you will see stars. Stars are all of the little lights you see in the sky. There are many, many stars. There are so many that no one can count them all!

Stars are not all the same. Some are big. Some are small. Some give more light than others do. The sun is a star. It isn't the biggest one. But it is **closer** to our Earth than the others. That's why we see it so well.

Stars *(cont.)*

Directions: Fill in the bubble next to the right answer.

1. In the night sky there are many

(a) moons.

(b) stars.

2. What happens first?

(a) You see the stars in the sky.

(b) The sun goes down.

3. What does the sun send to Earth?

(a) light

(b) storms

4. *Closer* means

(a) nearer.

(b) bigger.

5. Picture a night when you can see many stars. What is *not* in the sky?

(a) the moon

(b) thick clouds

Becoming Farmers

Long, long ago people did not know how to grow food. So they looked for fruits and nuts. They hunted and ate animals. The animals moved around. So the people had to move around, too. At night they looked for a cave to stay in. When they couldn't find one, they often got cold and wet.

Then people found out that if they put seeds in the ground, plants would grow. Then they could eat the plants or their seeds. This let the people stay in one place. They made homes and grew **crops**. They stored up food, too. They lived longer.

Becoming Farmers *(cont.)*

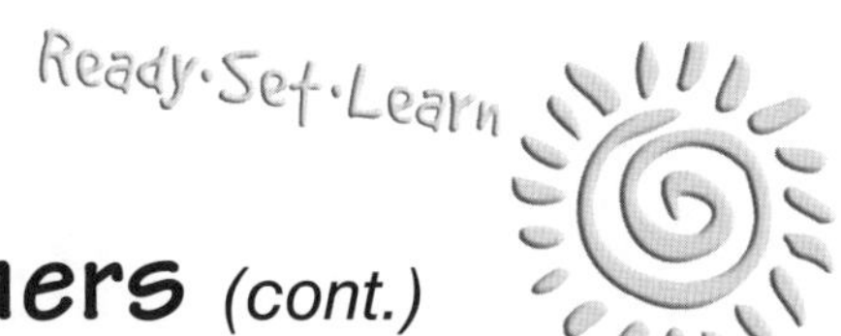

Directions: Fill in the bubble next to the right answer.

1. After people became farmers, they

ⓐ had a longer life than when they moved with the animals.

ⓑ had a shorter life than when they moved with the animals.

2. What happened first?

ⓐ People stayed in one place.

ⓑ People went where the animals went.

3. Why did people follow the animals?

ⓐ They needed to eat the animals for food.

ⓑ They felt bored.

4. What was a good thing about learning to farm?

ⓐ The people could save food.

ⓑ The people stopped eating animals.

5. Picture the people inside the caves. What gives them light?

ⓐ a flashlight

ⓑ a fire

Bruises

You bump your arm hard. You do not get cut. Your skin does not break. Still, you get a bruise. Your skin turns blue-black. What is a bruise? Why does your skin turn blue-black?

Blood flows in your body. It flows through tubes. Tubes that carry blood are called blood vessels. Some are big. Some tubes are tiny. The tiny tubes are called capillaries.

Living things are made of cells. Cells are like building blocks. They are the smallest building block of living things. Your body has lots of cells. It has many kinds of cells. You have bone cells. You have skin cells. You have lots of blood cells. Most of your blood cells are red blood cells. Red blood cells make your blood look red.

When you get bumped, you may not get cut. Still, you may hurt some capillaries. Some may break. Blood leaks from the capillaries. You bleed under your skin. When blood cells leak from the capillaries, they die. When the cells die, they turn blue-black. We see the blue-black color. We call the blue-black color a bruise.

Your body absorbs the dead blood cells. When something is absorbed, it is taken in. It is made part of itself. Fresh blood absorbs the dead blood cells. It takes many days. The bruise changes color. It changes color as the fresh blood absorbs the dead cells. It changes from blue-black to purple. It changes from purple to yellow. Finally, the bruise is gone. All the dead blood cells have been absorbed.

 48

Bruises *(cont.)*

Directions: Fill in the bubble next to the right answer.

1. What are living things made of?
- ⓐ blood
- ⓑ cells
- ⓒ vessels
- ⓓ capillaries

2. This story is mainly about
- ⓐ cells.
- ⓑ blood.
- ⓒ bruises.
- ⓓ capillaries.

3. If your bruise is yellow, it means that
- ⓐ your capillaries are leaking.
- ⓑ you are bleeding under the skin.
- ⓒ soon the bruise will change to blue-black.
- ⓓ most of the dead blood cells have been absorbed.

4. Which statement is true?
- ⓐ Vessels and capillaries are cells.
- ⓑ You do not have many blood vessels.
- ⓒ When you get a bruise, you cut your skin.
- ⓓ Red blood cells make your blood look red.

5. Think about how the word *tiny* relates to *small*. Which words relate in the same way?
- ⓐ many : lots
- ⓑ blood : red
- ⓒ bump : bruise
- ⓓ yellow : color

Blind and Deaf

Helen Keller was born on June 27, 1880. She was a happy baby. Then, Helen got sick. Helen got a fever. It hurt her ears. Helen became deaf. She could not hear.

Think about how you learn to talk. You listen. You learn to say what other people say. Helen could not hear. She could not listen. She could not learn to talk. The high fever also hurt Helen's eyes. Helen became blind. She could not see.

Helen was not happy. She became wild. She hit. She screamed. She threw things. She hurt people.

Helen's parents found a teacher. The teacher was named Annie Sullivan. Annie did not let Helen hit. She did not let her break or throw things. Annie taught Helen how to talk. Helen was deaf. She was blind. How could Annie teach her how to talk?

Annie made signs with her fingers. She used the signs to spell words. She made the signs in Helen's hand. At first, Helen did not know what the signs meant. Annie did not give up. She took Helen to a water pump. Annie pumped. Water came out. Helen felt the water. At the same time, Annie signed. She signed w-a-t-e-r. Then, Helen knew!

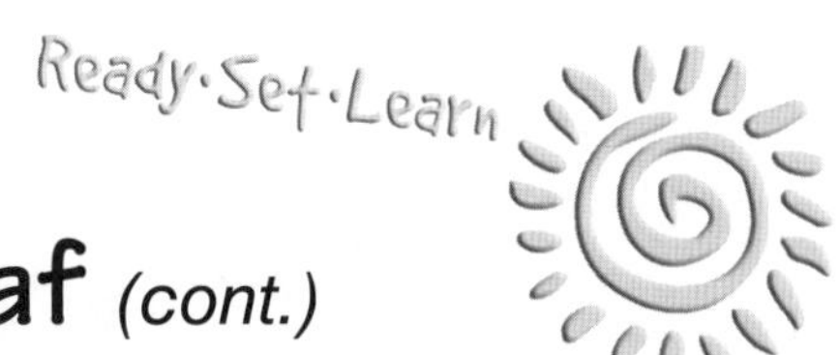

Blind and Deaf *(cont.)*

Directions: Fill in the bubble next to the right answer.

1. In the story, how did Helen learn to talk?
  ⓐ by looking at people make signs
  ⓑ by listening to what people said
  ⓒ by feeling words spelled into her hand

2. This story is mainly about
  ⓐ how to talk with signs.
  ⓑ a girl who was blind and deaf.
  ⓒ what a high fever did to a girl.

3. Why did Helen become wild?
  ⓐ She was unhappy because she could not talk.
  ⓑ She was unhappy because her sister was born.
  ⓒ She was unhappy because her teacher made finger signs.

4. What month was Helen born in?
  ⓐ June   ⓒ April
  ⓑ July   ⓓ August

5. Think about how the word *eye* relates to *see*. Which words relate in the same way?
  ⓐ ear : deaf   ⓒ ear : hear
  ⓑ eye : ears   ⓓ eye : blind

Better Than Gold

King Midas loved gold. He thought gold was the most important thing in the world. He had a lot of gold. He wanted more. One day, a man said to King Midas, "I will grant you one wish." When you grant something, you give what is asked for.

King Midas knew what he wanted. He wanted gold. He said, "I want to turn everything I touch into gold." The man granted the wish. King Midas was very happy. He touched grass. The grass turned to gold. He touched flowers. The flowers turned to gold. Everything King Midas touched turned to gold.

King Midas got hungry. He picked up his fork. The fork turned to gold. King Midas put food in his mouth. The food turned to gold! King Midas could not eat. King Midas had a child. She ran to her father. When she touched him, she turned to gold.

King Midas cried, "I am sad. My heart is broken. Gold cannot mend my broken heart. Gold cannot fill my hungry belly." After King Midas spoke, the man came back. He said he would grant one more wish. King Midas wished for everything to go back the way it was before. King Midas hugged his child. He said, "My heart is mended. You are worth more than gold. Now, let's eat!"

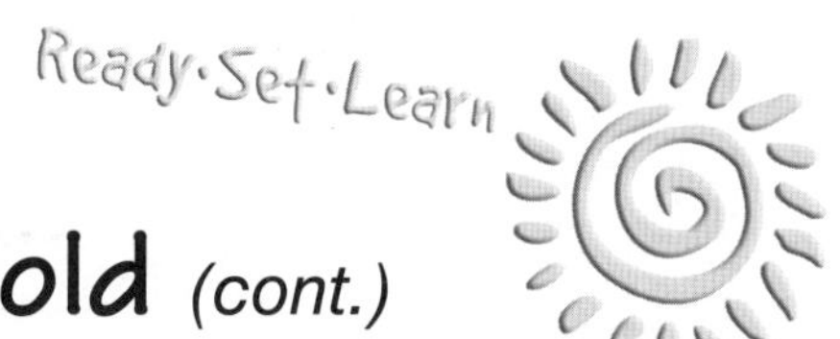

Better Than Gold *(cont.)*

Directions: Fill in the circle next to the correct answer.

1. What, according to the story, are the two most important things in the world?

   (a) gold and wishes
   (b) children and food
   (c) grass and flowers

2. When you grant something, you

   (a) mend a broken heart.
   (b) turn things to gold.
   (c) give what is asked for.

3. This story is mainly about

   (a) a story with a lesson about wishing.
   (b) a story with a lesson about the world.
   (c) a story with a lesson about what is important.

4. In the story, what did King Midas turn to gold first?

   (a) food   (b) grass
   (c) a chair   (d) flowers

5. Think about how the word *broken* relates to *mended*. What words relate in the same way?

   (a) sad : happy   (b) chair : table
   (c) lesson : story   (d) golden : touch

The First Step

The day was July 20th. The year was 1969. Neil Armstrong stepped out onto the moon. It had taken him three days to get there. He had to wear a spacesuit. He had to wear a suit because there was no air on the moon. There was no water. No one had ever gone to the moon before. Neil was the first man on the moon.

Neil did something. He did it right away. He did it as soon as he stepped out. What did Neil do? He took some lunar soil. Lunar soil is ground. It is ground from the moon. Lunar soil is rocky. It is dusty. Neil put the lunar soil in a bag. He put the bag in a pocket. The pocket was special. It was in his spacesuit. It was made just for the lunar soil.

Why did Neil take lunar soil? No one had ever been to the moon before. Scientists did not know what would happen. What if Neil had to leave the moon quickly? What if he had to leave before he could find out things for the scientists? Neil picked up the soil first. He did it so that if he had to come back quickly, he would not be empty-handed. Scientists could look at the rocks. They could study them. They could learn about the moon.

The First Step *(cont.)*

Directions: Fill in the circle next to the correct answer.

1. This story is mainly about
  ⓐ big and small craters.
  ⓑ scientists and lunar soil.
  ⓒ Neil Armstrong and the moon.

2. How long did it take Neil to get to the moon?
  ⓐ one day   ⓑ 20 years
  ⓒ three days   ⓓ 1969 years

3. Think about how the word *mountain* relates to *snowy*. Which words relate in the same way?
  ⓐ step : out   ⓑ rock : pocket
  ⓒ spacesuit : air   ⓓ moon : rocky

4. What is not true about the first step on the moon?
  ⓐ The ground was wet.
  ⓑ It happened on July 20th.
  ⓒ It happened in 1969.
  ⓓ Neil Armstrong took the first step.

5. Which answer is in the right order?
  ⓐ Neil put on a spacesuit; he got soil; he stepped out.
  ⓑ Neil stepped out; he got soil; he put soil in his pocket.
  ⓒ Neil went to the moon; he stepped out; he put on a spacesuit.

Sharks

A shark has lots more teeth than you do. Some sharks have hundreds of teeth. Sharks lose more teeth than you, too. In fact, sharks lose their teeth all the time. Feel your teeth. They are set firmly into your jaw. When something is firmly set, it does not move. It is fixed. A shark's teeth are not firmly set.

Losing a tooth does not bother a shark. Why not? Sharks have many new teeth. The new teeth are in the jaws. The new teeth come out fast. How fast? It takes only 24 hours for some teeth to grow in. A shark can have new teeth in just one day!

Most sharks are born alive. They are born ready to hunt. Nurse sharks have about 20 to 30 babies at a time. Nurse-shark babies are about one foot (30 centimeters) long when they are born. Great White shark babies are bigger. Some are four-and-a-half feet (137 centimeters) long!

Other sharks are hatched out of eggs. The eggs are not hard. The eggs are thick. They are rubbery. The thick, rubbery eggs protect the babies inside. Most of the eggs have strings on them. The strings catch on seaweed. The strings catch on coral. They keep the eggs from floating away.

Sharks *(cont.)*

Directions: Fill in the circle next to the correct answer.

1. This story is mainly about
- ⓐ eggs.
- ⓑ pups.
- ⓒ teeth.
- ⓓ sharks.

2. Why are shark eggs thick and rubbery?
- ⓐ to catch on seaweed
- ⓑ to firmly fix strings
- ⓒ to protect the babies inside

3. Think about how the word *tooth* relates to *teeth*. Which words relate in the same way?
- ⓐ babies : baby
- ⓑ shark : sharks
- ⓒ eggs : strings
- ⓓ seaweed : coral

4. From the story you can tell that
- ⓐ all sharks are born alive.
- ⓑ one baby shark is born at a time.
- ⓒ there is more than one kind of shark.

5. When something is firm, it
- ⓐ does not move.
- ⓑ is thick and rubbery.
- ⓒ grows back in 24 hours.

Steel

Steel is strong. Steel is light. We make many things out of steel. Bridges need to be strong and light. We make many bridges out of steel. We use steel in tall buildings. The strong, light steel helps hold up the building. We use steel in cars. We make tools out of steel. We make pots and pans. We make spoons and knives. We use steel every day.

Where do we get steel? Is it a plant? Is it a rock? Steel is not a plant. We cannot grow steel. It is not alive. Steel is not a rock. We cannot just find it. We have to make it.

Steel is a special metal. We make it from iron. Iron is found in a rock called iron ore. We mine iron ore. When we mine something, we dig it out.

The iron ore is sent to a steel plant. The steel plant has big ovens. Some ovens are used to heat the iron ore. The ovens get so hot that the iron ore melts. It turns from a solid into a liquid. The liquid iron is poured into more ovens. These ovens blow oxygen through the melted iron. The oxygen burns out everything but the iron.

The iron is changed to steel. We mix things into the melted iron. When we add different things, we make different kinds of steel. What do we do with the hot steel? We pour some steel into molds. We form it into blocks. We pass some steel between rollers. The rollers shape the steel into flat pieces. We can make things from the blocks. We can make things from the flat pieces.

Steel *(cont.)*

Directions: Fill in the circle next to the correct answer.

1. Which statement is true?
- ⓐ We can mine steel.
- ⓑ We can grow steel.
- ⓒ Steel is made from iron.

2. This story is mainly about
- ⓐ metal.
- ⓑ steel.
- ⓒ bridges.
- ⓓ iron ore.

3. Which answer is in the correct order?
- ⓐ mine iron ore, melt it, pour steel into molds
- ⓑ mine iron ore, melt it, send it to a steel plant
- ⓒ send iron ore to a steel plant, melt it, mine it

4. What do some ovens blow through the melted iron?
- ⓐ metal
- ⓑ oxygen
- ⓒ rollers
- ⓓ iron ore

**5. Think about how the word *iron* relates to *metal.*
Which words relate in the same way?**
- ⓐ steel : solid
- ⓑ steel : liquid
- ⓒ iron ore : mine
- ⓓ iron ore : rock

Abraham Lincoln

Directions: Read the passage below. Answer the questions at the bottom of the page.

Abraham Lincoln was born on February 12, 1809. As a child, he loved to read books. He borrowed books from other people.   Abraham Lincoln became the 16th president on March 4, 1861. The Civil War began while he was president. It lasted for four years. During the war, Lincoln worked to keep our country together. Abraham Lincoln was killed five days after the war ended. The people of the United States were very sad. They had lost their president. Lincoln will always be remembered. Many people believe that he was one of our greatest presidents. The Lincoln Memorial honors him today.

1. When was Abraham Lincoln born?________________________

2. When did Abraham Lincoln become president of the United States? ____

3. What did Lincoln do during the war?________________________

____

Answer Key

Page 4
1. cake
2. oven
3. person

Page 5
1. grass
2. plants

Page 6
1. dog
2. pet

Page 7
1. Jack and Jill
2. He fell and broke his crown.

Page 8
1. tub
2. bug

Page 9
1. reads a story
2. about his/her day
3. with sweet dreams

Page 10
1. b
2. a
3. c
4. a

Page 11
1. b
2. a
3. c

Page 13
1. a
2. b
3. a
4. b
5. a

Page 15
1. a
2. b
3. b
4. a
5. a

Page 17
1. a
2. b
3. a
4. a
5. b

Page 19
1. b
2. a
3. a
4. a
5. b

Page 21
1. b
2. b
3. a
4. b
5. a

Page 23
1. b
2. a
3. b
4. b
5. b

Page 25
1. a
2. a
3. b
4. b
5. b

Page 27
1. b
2. b
3. a
4. b
5. a

Page 29
1. b
2. b
3. b
4. a
5. b

Page 31
1. b
2. b
3. a
4. a
5. a

Answer Key *(cont.)*

Page 33
1. a
2. b
3. b
4. a
5. a

Page 35
1. a
2. b
3. b
4. b
5. a

Page 37
1. a
2. b
3. a
4. b
5. a

Page 39
1. a
2. b
3. a
4. b
5. a

Page 41
1. b
2. a
3. b
4. b
5. a

Page 43
1. b
2. b
3. a
4. b
5. a

Page 45
1. b
2. b
3. a
4. a
5. b

Page 47
1. a
2. b
3. a
4. a
5. b

Page 49
1. b
2. c
3. d
4. d
5. a

Page 51
1. c
2. b
3. a
4. a
5. c

Page 53
1. b
2. c
3. c
4. b
5. a

Page 55
1. c
2. c
3. d
4. a
5. b

Page 57
1. d
2. c
3. b
4. c
5. a

Page 59
1. c
2. b
3. a
4. b
5. d

Page 60
1. February 12, 1809
2. March 4, 1861
3. He worked to keep our country together.

This Award
Is Presented To

____

for

★ Doing Your Best

★ Trying Hard

★ Not Giving Up

★ Making a
Great Effort